SWEET ILLUSIONS

TANMAY DUBEY

Copyright © Tanmay Dubey
All Rights Reserved.

ISBN 978-1-68509-473-7

This book has been published with all efforts taken to make the material error-free after the consent of the author. However, the author and the publisher do not assume and hereby disclaim any liability to any party for any loss, damage, or disruption caused by errors or omissions, whether such errors or omissions result from negligence, accident, or any other cause.

While every effort has been made to avoid any mistake or omission, this publication is being sold on the condition and understanding that neither the author nor the publishers or printers would be liable in any manner to any person by reason of any mistake or omission in this publication or for any action taken or omitted to be taken or advice rendered or accepted on the basis of this work. For any defect in printing or binding the publishers will be liable only to replace the defective copy by another copy of this work then available.

To the Muses, hope this is worth your blessings

Contents

Preface .... *vii*

1. Leaded Destruction 1
2. Sharpened Sunshine 3
3. Expelled Abyss 4
4. Rushed Blood 5
5. Meant Dream 7
6. Blink 9
7. Wrecked Persuit Of Emptiness 10
8. Thread 12
9. Endless Falling 14
10. Portrayel Of Inner Self 16
11. Blurred 18
12. Sudden Stab 19
13. Venomous Element 20
14. Sky Of Agony 21
15. Wrecked Past 22
16. Unwritten Belonging 23
17. Questions Unleashed 24
18. Portrayed Breaths 26
19. Blinding Curtain 27
20. Unwoven Carpet 29
21. Inches Of Chaos 30
22. A Dot To Remember 31
23. Unjust 32

Contents

24. Sealed Misery — 33
25. Strange Lightning — 34
26. Seethed Pain — 35
27. Covered Breath — 36
28. Scribled — 37
29. Dark Fruit — 38
30. An Inch Of Illusion — 39
31. Smothered Memory — 41
32. Unopened — 42
33. Dark Orthodox — 44
34. Blinded — 45
Thank You Note — 47

Preface

The book "SWEET ILLUSIONS" is a bubble of the existence of a 18 year old kid which is presented in a poetic manner. The author has touched the catharsis which was hidden for centuries, we all perceive the actuality of life but we are unknown to the buried illusion which we deny by the fear which we are the only ones to understand.

Well my friend, this book will take you to the journey of illusions of immense thoughts

and all those moments which is felt by the author in the peculiar realms of every single feeling

so sit back, relax and feel every illusion as if you are living in it.

1. Leaded destruction

*Thoughts threatening the dreams
undefined existence and darkness unseen
unopened realms of shivering shields.
A woven puppet dreading in reality
Breaths decaying the state of solidity
a palm was opened
and darkness was sealed
in every bloodied nail
what threatened was a blink
the fear of reality stabbing
so fine that even mirrors couldn't hide
every path was dark enough to fall
every road of sorrow turned bitter
and every bliss shined like a rusted pole
pieces of paranoia walked with wrapped miseries
and darkness was raised like a toast
beneath the perfected hours of broken dreams
screams unleashed their breaths
and evil fell in a ray of peculiar sunshine*

SWEET ILLUSIONS

2. Sharpened Sunshine

Beloved were those dreams
in the mornings of vanished screams
the tress held their silence
the smell of mud crafted a lie
a step, a blink, a power.
the game of seconds damaged the stars from nowhere
and portrayed a thin layer of past
It was too late to hold, the time of solitude
and escapism from smothered warmth
wrapped with all the lies and denials
fine grains of calamity with a fruit of betrayal
banded with unwanted filth
all one had was nothing but air to breath
and bitterest of all
blinking beneath the shallow abyss
the abyss of blinded rivers.

3. Expelled abyss

The era of inches of sunshine
and laughs among frozen clocks
what frighted the embraced darkness
expelled the silence beneath bitter skies
the inches of rottenness
and elements of dazzled dreams
sheds a tear in agony
and bards weeping in blissed realms
where the knowledge blesses
and stabs the veins of burnt faces
where shadows play in nothingness
and breaths rise in warm shields
from elements to swords and expressed words to
forbidden kings
it remained untouched and followed by none.

4. Rushed blood

Dreaded sunshine in the melancholic breeze
crippled darkness in the deepest soul
heavenly steps of paled gems
being bitten and bittered
from an erased beginning of choked miseries
spelled seas brightened the past in threatened clouds
erased memories of agony
and embraced thunders of wrecked smiles
filthy years of questioned anatomy
emanated by none and expelled in dirt
aching veins and warm tears
frozen bliss of shining moon
the time when soul glanced rather than gazing
and every chant was silent
the truth was burnt in crumbled pages,
it neglected to burn in tears
it melted the glory
it halted in every breath
yet enslaved in the bitterest agony.

5. Meant dream

Heavenly were the steps
And what was left was bitten beauty
Bitter was the breeze and so were the shadows
Like a incarnated flower plowed and planted in the agony
of warmth
the mesmerized corners sighed for the last time
and the darkened moon crisped behind
and every breeze collapsed under smothering trees
the eyes were crumpled
Vanished like burned books
Tied with bruises with their forbidden lies
With the unspoken dreams of thy.
some had bliss, some were threatened
but the feeling of self
when the wraith stabbed
and the shivering blink bleeding
weeping for the savior
the weaker it informed the stronger it stabbed
in the deepest river of unknown skies
in which warmth was questioned

with petrified souls.

6. Blink

Unheard shores of darkness
what belonged, questioned
What was handed was undreamed
every time the eyes blinked they felt like a meadow
in a volcano yet the breeze was ultimate
breaths weakened, and past abandoned
and the moon crumbled in melting eyes
forbidden suns hid in the shivering umbrella
they say it takes years to feel a will
but when the hidden self seek
every element rathers to rise
what fell was the glory of sunshine
What fed were the depths of the forbidden sky
and with an inkling of life,
i troubled the veins.
A burning eye spoked and blinked
the seasons of miseries felt a blinded abyss.

7. Wrecked persuit of emptiness

The catharsis and dreams of blurred abyss
it's a will to dread in the silence
songs and poems are woven
the time of touched freedom
it expels those stabbed thoughts and betrays the sorrow and
sings melancholy when it rains
the time when agony was unleashed
and ended when bliss birthed and counted its breaths
It's a passion which none could endure
cold breeze, and halted dreams
silence rushed as blood in a human
It left at its loudest
and when the sun shined and when the birds sang
the gloom vanished it's inches like an erased poetry
and left the feeling of truth
the understanding among.
Reached it's place and stabbed the instrument of thoughts
and truth came out of a pink gloom.

TANMAY DUBEY

8. Thread

It was a play of faded skies
It was a stabbing warmth
It is the portrayal of wraith
nurtured in bruised thoughts
with peculiar faced fiends
the feeling among was irony
the foolish was once throned
and the wise were expelled far away
with the thoughts which dazzled
the wraith which wrecked
and the glory remained as a stamp
every sun stabbed
every night healed
the loop was infinite
endless like abyss
time by time the rubber thrust
with the curses of blinded innocence
the bones were unhealed
yet the subconscious was about to feel.
The breeze rushed in the veins

like it sways in unknown clouds
and no bard was ever written
in the destiny of the coldest nights

9. Endless Falling

Fruitful verses start ugly
shivering existence rise peacefully
it's a realm that is unnamed
meadows, skies, and deaf tress belong here
and I forbid to name
they ask why with the interest of an old cat
don't call it beauty like sold poets
Oh, don't be a puppet mate!
let me open this rusted door
I have waited for so long
given is the mercy
the pain of faded skies are now nothing
every breeze is warm
not tender, just warm.
I understand your agony
but this path is a silent road
and no one is on your side in which silence melts rotten
eyes
and stars sneak tremendous
it is an abyss of numbness and untouched sun

in which dreams are thrust and thunders are unleashed
it is a breath of enslaved sorrows.

10. Portrayel of inner self

Like a thread in the ocean
like a feather in the sky
like a fear dreading by,
The warmth and
the bliss of adoring its very existence
the thirst of the broken wind
the troubling glory of the blooded heaven
Oh I can see it
Oh I can discern the depth
the charm of the sprinkled moon
the calmness in those swaying clouds
the breeze forbidding the reincarnation
slew halts and dreams of buried sorrow
detached clouds and unbroken windows
Songs and the travel through mysteries of mankind
no, I don't defend,
no, I don't cherish.
all the pleasures are unborrowed
and with all the darkness among
I stay.

TANMAY DUBEY

11. Blurred

The portrayal of the blurred abyss
threatens the imperfections of the inner self
It pretends to fly, darkness fades the silence
and raised a crippled moon
heaven melted volcanos
the coldest of evenings vanished
the breaths bleated the skies of burnt thoughts.
Rusted bulbs gazed the blooded corners
And roots inhaled the bliss of minutes.
Quills crisped in the eyes of blinded poets
rain shivered beneath the spells and lies
when the devil sipped the veins
the nights thrust the obeyed dreams
and the reality was choked unkind.

12. Sudden Stab

Wraith existence and crimson lies
Heavenly were the steps
and what was left was bitten beauty
bitter were the trees and so were the shadows
like an incarnated flower plowed
and planted in the agony of warmth
the mesmerized corners sighed for the last time
and the darkest moon crisped behind
the sun came up and clouds were red
and every breeze collapsed under smothering trees
the eyes crumbled
vanished like burned books
tied with the bruises of their forbidden lies
and unspoken dreams of thy
a sudden thrust in a numb sleep
curtains turned into ashes with stabbed betrayal
with a taste of warm rain of a hellish December

13. Venomous element

It's the trimmed anger
And unshivered clocks of thy
elementary breaths in the endless skies
hours were the coldest for the sake of mankind
ashes were brightened
tasted trouble for every vein
inches of bliss faded
and every god fed the lie
every smile shortened
every breath burned pleasantly
as time flies like a thread in the sky
none questioned the glory of thy

14. Sky of agony

Glanced dirt of a golden cave
Unopened and unforgiven mysteries
Like hunters kill a bear with filthy souls
Blood and past admired and chocked.
And what is left is the water,
the water which belongs to us,
the water they made us drink with our wreaked arms
Yet the beliefs were burdened And the sun was bleated
And every breath ached
Every corner was burned with lost dignity
With the laughs of the deepest unconscious mind
The divided realm remained unspoken
And the left pieces were enslaved with warm swords hoping
the image will burn the blinded curtain.
and leaves the traces of brotherhood among.

15. Wrecked past

*Faded stories and darkened gems
a brutal rhyme to bruised thoughts
Behold was the incarnation
So were the unhidden poems
Oaths were broken and scare shined
the breeze was forbidden and nothing was behind
every cold arrow was stabbed in cold veins
and blooded rivers dried and tress talked
their roots were hidden, burned in cold realms.
As a warrior of darkness shoves the feathers in the closets
of hell
Those chapters of unknown screams crossed the bridges of
agony and opened themselves inside the ashes
of cold lies and futile fruits
and what was left was silence, minutes, hours, years,wars
and depths of known and unknown
In the flaked universe of ended thoughts.*

16. Unwritten belonging

Some places burn empty
some tears thirst alone
when the sunshine dreads
the stars bleed in the finest line
and when a diminished soul melt
no bard steals a slice of truth
there swords rust
their eyes blink rotten
there leashed tongs shiver in the dark
and breeze turn unkind
the faces of warm rhymes
stabs in a feral catastrophe
the venom inside laughs
the shining insult and glory of filthy souls
hands tendered waves in selfish deapths
who sips and spreads the same bitter aura.

17. Questions unleashed

Debirs of thy
In my dark reality
which a weeping warmth couldn't perceive
sudden sunshine came with its blooded pleasures
to make those tears venomous
It thrust the very breeze
which resisted the pain
It calmed the damage with a crumbled paper
tender yet futile.
A thin ray of light feeling the paled eyes
with a reckless existence.
Brightened rooms, cold swords
and warmth in a burnt silence
sudden bow to ended conscious
warm breaths and injured lips
bruises inside.
what to feel what forbid to
a fine line of sunshine
or crippled pieces of a gloomy heaven?

18. Portrayed breaths

Shallow strengthened tears dreaded
sketched past blurred
volcanic voids turned blind
falling fears smiled
as if forbidden sunshine would whine
the crimson valley melted off the crown
call it fortunes of lies
and threats of the kindest smiles
bittered veins exhaust beneath rotten eyes
nature stabbed in a scribbled death
portrayed ashes smiled and hanged
suck the marrow of warm darkness
inhale the vein of blooded nails
poke the eyes with your finest sword
and sing a rhyme from seething diaries

19. Blinding Curtain

Scared scares and blurry winds
Dreaded past and a savory end
depths to endless questions
reckless ground and threatening suns
. To smile, to feel, to breath
What fetishes to believe?
I answer to none.
Semi crunch to perceive and a leashed vein to feel.
Just to say what troubles and what heals
I begin to ache near the sun
asking none while answering some.
Trees, mountains, rivers are somewhere untouched near the forbidden sky.
But what is the element which imperfects thy?
What thy perceive is the inkling of the unknown realm.
The knight shall remain under the tree of cherishing chants
, shall remain bleating the weak with endless glory.
And the realm remains with the name of light,
unspoken and forgotten with the rumors which vanish the reality inch by inch.

SWEET ILLUSIONS

20. Unwoven carpet

A fiend darkens the portrayal
it blurs the soul with a curled thrust
and when the lies seal the truth
every breath bows agony
and abyss closes their doors
the almighty blinks sorrow
and every pen writes blooded letters
sudden swords stab in the coldest of bloods
with tiny demons laughing in glory
unnamed skies bleat
and known souls enslaves the ashes
and breathes the glasses of freedom
in the fire which they mesmerize

21. Inches of chaos

Shall I care to thrust agony
while thee stab in a fruitful dream
and cover the story with breathing coins
the diary which wrote an unconscious letter
which floated in the air which poisoned
and songs that curved a burnt road
it was vivid and dazzled
and bliss which crisped the ends
no word would stand by
and no spell would purify
and when the breeze sway a leaf
it thrust the marrow of warmth
and the glory of self
burry the woven play
and the silence reaches to none.

22. A dot to remember

Thou seething behind the finest tree
in the moment breeze turn peculiar
and mornings smells like betrayal
the most vivid past smother
and darkness spreads the perfect lie
with a blinded glance
the oceans talk bitter
and with an inkling of a forbidden sunshine
every bird breathe agony
and the art of laminating darkness stays
as if a blooded knife
would leave it's half
in the emptiest of the souls.

23. Unjust

Here I am in this dark silent abyss
fingers shiver, eyes are numb
I am thrust enough
every blink is peculiar
the finest mist enslave its abuse
the crows glance rottenness
nature seems bitter
the locked thoughts pretend blur
the inches curve blind
the elements expel unkindly
and filth chokes unconscious
dreams taste the marrow of misery
the vivid river sip the warmest sorrow
and the coldest breath dreads for the morrow
time incarnates the deepest soul.
The stabbed lie
rise among the beginning
the village seems bright.

24. Sealed misery

*I shall carve the endings of nothingness
when thou weep in fainted sunshine
and the tress synchronize tremendously
the mighty breeze scream darkness
and the coldest of rivers sing
when November breathe the kindest foe
and abstracts wove a slight dream
seconds before it sleds
it barks universe,
sheds a tear to befriend mankind
and buries the bruised
no light expels emptiness
no darkness destruct
and the bitterest of bliss
gaze the narrowest sky
where flames light crumbled candles.*

25. Strange lightning

The melancholic breeze transcends
It leaves the silence beneath
the skies halt
the breeze shines agony
and darkness births misery
it dreams the finest abyss of emptiness
it wakes from the bitterest sleep
and baffles every breath
glances to embrace the sorrow
with defined depths of craved means
and swords bowing the equivalent
in the deadliest rows of beginning
the era of the slightest venom
held the breaths of rotten snow
it upbrings the voids
with the shallowest thought
and rains calmness
amongst the authority of immense.

26. Seethed pain

A quill questioned
a rooted beginning stabbing blinded needles
it tasted the filth of an unread past
with trimmed pages
from a pleasureful diary
and crimson verses of numbed existence.
Sudden rows of crippled homage
Invaded by untouched foes
with seething breaths
and torn oaths
with endless stabs
in which elements endure threatening abstracts
which dies within the life of self and erased identities
it expels the meadows
from the very moment of bliss
it forbids to count the ends
and slit the peculiar norm
in the existence which screams alone.

27. Covered breath

Shedding a tear of glory
with unvivid inkling
the towns civilized by rust
I ask for will
they birth for misery
accuses and faces
heard and seen from the nearest sky
it is in the incarnation
beliefs and denial
I fright to name them
they are embraced and expelled
beneath the bitterest sun
its laughable and fabled in the same boat
the voids of calamity
in the most tremendous shadow
enslaved in dazzled forests
which transcends infinitely.

28. Scribled

The farthest quill of a dark poet
writes rotten bliss of beauty
It melts the brightest of fiends
It borrows a melodious end
It incarnates the bruised silence
in the bluest of the moon.
It dreads to question
It bows to the gloom
It smothers lone
It steals its will
with the evilest sword
it bleeds for none
but injures many
it travels to illusions
but has tasted none.

29. Dark fruit

As the crimson moon exhaust
and fears breathe nothingness
with the violent blink
it bursts and forbids to dwell
the arrogance among
cripple the agony
the fruited root
to the forest of melting numbness
partially incarnating
the literalist of all
to decaying the marrow of death
with chants of the abyss
it transcends the bruises
to the shelters of filthiest fire
and they bow to evil.

30. An Inch of illusion

It's the sweetest portrayal
In which poured silence worships peace
It makes the warmest honey
and angels sing to wish
it is vivid as the misery of bruise
and gratifies the soul
where validations are dust
and are craved by the breaths of none
it is the fog of kindness
and fruit of endless shelters
in which no door exists
and no one weeps for freedom
because they are breathed
by the only
which is damaged
and ought to be hidden
and gaze at the beauty of the sweetest illusions
Now, swallow and swim
the time has come...

31. Smothered memory

The feeling was discerned
I endured the innocence
the fiends laughed
thou breathed hypocrisy
and seething in front
leading the lives of maybes
and blinking in the loops of memories
I played my part
I ran out
I accused none
I questioned many.
while sipping the faults
and feeling the bright
now the dreams I meant
was unfelt by me
and the memory thrust
and left the joy among

32. Unopened

Run. To a clouded blanket!
with the slightest of fear
I say scream!
Love the loop, my friend
get bruised on a sunny day
and puke memories
I am your blinded shoulder
I have seen enough
I say die once in a mist
and live to end the eyebrows
I am sealed
yet I perceive
the darkest screams
which I screamed
in the forbidden years
in which, bliss blushes far away
and darkness chokes the kindest of smiles
and the warmest of the worlds
ache near the brightest sun.

33. Dark orthodox

As the moon burn brutal
and particles remain unchanged
from the farthest of all
to the nearest end
it sparks the silence
and lands dread again
they fascinate morrow
and smother today
to bear the thought
and eclipse the bruise
it hides
it screams nothingness
and breathe the glitteriest deaths
beneath the crimson clouds
and expel the bleated bards
to seethe for none.

34. Blinded

In the simulations of subconscious swords
thy trims the silence among none
it breathes the blisses of materials
and screams the suffering near some
I shall unwire but questions come.
They behold blind
and slit some more
the abstracts of the bloodiest stoic
in the nature of hellish horses
they crucify the silence after wars
and brings sorrow among
like flowers from meadows
it laughs agony
and shed the tears of joy
but is the only left
among the breezes of none.

Thank You Note

Dear reader, I am grateful that you decided to pick up this book and read it as we know we live in a world where reading is a fading habit, this surely means a lot. I wish you all the success and prosperity.
Thank you
contact : theuninkingpenpublishing@gmail.com

www.ingramcontent.com/pod-product-compliance
Lightning Source LLC
LaVergne TN
LVHW011859060526
838200LV00054B/4429